ARCHITECTING A SUSTAINABLE DIGITAL FUTURE

Satya Prakash

Qurate
quratebooks.com

Architecting A Sustainable Digital Future
Satya Prakash

Published in 2025

© Published by

urate
quratebooks.com

Qurate Books Pvt. Ltd.
Goa 403523, India
www.quratebooks.com
Tel: 1800-210-6527,
Email: info@quratebooks.com

ISBN: 978-93-58985-60-3

✨ Note on Originality:

All content, insights, and quotes in this publication are original works by the author, Satya Prakash. Any similarity to external works is purely coincidental or used under fair use principles.

The inclusion of real-life stories, personal reflections, and professional methodologies is intended solely for educational and informational purposes. All references to individuals,

✨ Disclaimer on tool used

This book is intended for educational and professional reference purposes. All views expressed are those of the author and do not represent the official stance of any organization.

All product names, logos, brands, and trademarks mentioned in this publication — including but not limited to Microsoft, SAP, Oracle, Power BI, Eco Vadis, and CDP — are the property of their respective owners. Their inclusion herein does not imply affiliation, endorsement, sponsorship, or approval by the trademark holders.

Any references to proprietary tools or platforms are for illustrative purposes only, based on publicly available features and use cases at the time of writing.

The author has made every effort to ensure that information in this book is accurate and current. However, technology and sustainability practices evolve rapidly, and readers are encouraged to consult official sources for the latest updates.

✨ Preface

The future we're building must do more than scale. It must sustain.

As a Digital Architect, I once focused only on performance, optimization, and automation. But gradually, I began to see the broader picture — the unseen environmental cost of always-on infrastructure, energy-hungry systems, and short-sighted digital designs.

This book is a blueprint and a bridge — connecting cutting-edge technology with ecological responsibility.

Whether you are an engineer, architect, policymaker, or entrepreneur, I hope the insights in this book empower you to build solutions that are not just smart, but sustainable.

Because the future will be digital — but it must also be ethical, inclusive, and regenerative.

– Satya Prakash

2025

Contents

Chapter 1

My Journey – Architecting with Purpose"

From Gorakhpur to Bangalore

"I don't just build systems. I build value. I build the future."
I was born in **Gorakhpur**, a place rich in culture and humility — and grounded in values that shaped how I see the world. Growing up, I didn't dream of becoming a Digital Architect or working on global enterprise strategies. I simply wanted to build a meaningful career — one step at a time.

My journey began as a **MIS Executive**, working with reports, data, and repetitive manual processes. It was hands-on, and it gave me something foundational: an understanding of how systems work and how people interact with them. But more importantly, it taught me where inefficiencies live — and how they slow down progress.

Driven by curiosity and the urge to solve real problems, I moved into the world of **Robotic Process Automation (RPA)**. As an **RPA Developer**, I saw the potential to transform the repetitive into the intelligent. Automating processes wasn't just about saving time; it was about unlocking human potential for more strategic, creative work. I realized that automation wasn't the end — it was the beginning of smarter architecture.

Over time, my role grew into **Solution and Platform Architecture**, designing systems that scaled across geographies and industries. From optimizing operations to improving user experience, I became obsessed with systems thinking — how every digital decision ripples across performance, cost, and usability.

But something kept tugging at me. As I saw more data centers being spun up, devices being connected, and workloads being virtualized, a question grew louder in my mind:

> Are we building a smarter world or just a faster one?

The turning point came when I began deeply studying the **environmental footprint of digital systems** — energy consumption, hardware waste, carbon emissions, and more. I realized that while we were optimizing business outcomes, we were unintentionally contributing to climate risk.

That's when I transitioned — not by changing industries, but by expanding my purpose. I embraced the role of a **Sustainability Architect** — someone who ensures that digital innovation and ecological responsibility walk together. I began aligning technology choices not just with KPIs, but with **carbon impact, energy efficiency,** and **resource optimization.**

Today, as a **Digital Architect** working across **Enterprise Sustainability Strategy,** I bring together the best of both worlds — automation and ethics, performance and preservation, intelligence and intention.

This book is the story of that transformation — and a practical blueprint for others.

It's for every technologist who wonders how they can contribute to sustainability. For every leader who wants to align business growth with environmental responsibility. And for every young architect trying to design a career that doesn't just succeed — but matters.

Because sustainability isn't just a corporate goal. It's a personal commitment And architecture isn't just about designing systems — it's about designing the future we want to live in.

This isn't just a technical guide. It's a reminder to every professional who thinks they're too small to create global impact. If I can build a sustainability-first career from a small-town desk, **so can you**.

Because we are no longer just building digital systems.

We are **Architecting the future.**

Chapter 2

The Digital Shift in Industry

"Seeing Efficiency Beyond the Obvious"

I used to chase automation for speed. Now I architect for impact."

— **Satya Prakash**, Digital & Sustainability Architect

In my early years in digital transformation, success meant one thing: speed.

The faster a report ran, the quicker a bot executed a task, the better we felt. Automation was king, and every meeting I attended focused on how many hours we saved or how many FTEs we optimized. I was proud of what we delivered — and rightfully so. But somewhere along the way, **the numbers stopped inspiring me.**

I remember once automating a financial reconciliation process that ran across four countries. It was a massive success — processing thousands of records in minutes, replacing hours of human effort. Applause followed. Yet, that evening, I sat staring at my laptop wondering:

How much electricity did this consume?

How many systems are now running 24x7 because we just proved they can?

No one asked those questions. Not even me — until that moment.

That's when I realized something: **Digital transformation without sustainability is like flying blind.**

Yes, we moved fast. But were we moving in the right direction?

💡 The Digital Efficiency Trap

Digital tools have become the backbone of modern industry. From AI-based demand forecasting to IoT-enabled logistics, businesses now run on **data, algorithms, and real-time decision-making.** But with that speed comes a **hidden environmental cost.**

Let's break it down with examples I've seen firsthand:

- A global organization migrated their infrastructure to the cloud but forgot to switch off unused virtual machines — resulting in **millions of kilograms of avoidable CO_2** emissions every year.
- A manufacturing firm installed smart sensors for predictive maintenance but failed to integrate lifecycle power management — the devices consumed power 24/7, even when inactive.
- Teams celebrated dashboards and analytics, but no one ever asked, *"What's the carbon cost of this daily data refresh across 50 countries?"*

Efficiency without awareness can be deceptive. It's like celebrating faster cars without checking if they have brakes.

🧠 The Mindset Shift: From chapter to Accountability

The truth is, most digital professionals are not trained to think about sustainability. I wasn't. My education and certifications focused on throughput, optimization, ROI — never on **energy intensity, carbon output,** or **green architecture.**

That shift had to come from within.

I started asking questions at design meetings:

- *Can we schedule this batch to run when renewable energy is most available?*
- *Can we reduce refresh frequency or data granularity without harming insights?*
- *Can we include sustainability metrics as part of our KPIs?*

These weren't always easy conversations. But they were necessary and with each conversation, I saw a new version of digital transformation take shape — one that wasn't just smart or fast, but also **responsible**.

From Efficiency to Responsibility:

There was a time when digitization was seen as a badge of progress. Every organization wanted to "go digital," automate, and modernize. And rightly so — digital tools revolutionized speed, scale, and customer experience.

I witnessed that change firsthand.

I remember one of my early projects in a large organization where we transitioned hundreds of manual processes to automated workflows. The results were impressive: faster turnaround, fewer errors, reduced headcount for repetitive work. It was seen as a major win.

But as I sat in the after-action review meeting, celebrating those improvements, a thought quietly surfaced in my mind:

"If every new system we build increases energy demand, are we really solving the bigger problem?"

It's a question most people in tech don't stop to ask — but we must. Because the **digital shift,** while powerful, is not without its costs.

⇥⇥⇥⇥⇥⇥⇥

⚙ The Invisible Weight of Digital

When we think of environmental impact, we imagine factories or smoke stacks — not laptops, APIs, or cloud services. But in reality, the **digital ecosystem is one of the fastest-growing contributors to global carbon emissions.**

Let me share something real: in one enterprise project, we had 80+ bots running 24/7 across virtual machines. Nobody thought to shut them down at night. Each bot saved labor hours — but collectively, they consumed enough power to run a small office for weeks.

Multiply that by thousands of businesses. Now think about the data centers that support those bots, the air conditioning required to cool the servers, and the electricity drawn from fossil fuels. Suddenly, our automation doesn't feel so "lightweight" anymore.

→I→I→I→I→I→I→I

💡 The Misunderstood Progress

We often equate "digital" with "green." After all, a paperless office is better, right?

Yes — but only if the systems replacing paper are **efficient, monitored,** and **designed with intent.**

"True digital progress doesn't just move faster. It moves cleaner."

— Satya Prakash (© 2025)

That line is mine — and I say it with pride. Because I've learned that sustainable architecture isn't about avoiding digital change. It's about **guiding it consciously.**

→I→I→I→I→I→I→I

📉 What's Missing in Today's Digital Strategy?

1. **CO_2 Visibility** – Most IT teams have no idea what their infrastructure is emitting.
2. **Sustainability KPIs** – We track uptime, latency, SLA, but not energy draw or idle compute.
3. **Lifecycle Blindness** – Systems are built for launch, not longevity. No one plans decommissioning, renewability, or green sourcing.

4. **Cloud Myths** – Many assume the cloud is "clean" — but unless you're selecting green data centers, you're likely just outsourcing your emissions.

⇥⇥⇥⇥⇥⇥⇥

🌍 A Call to Shift the Shift

The digital shift changed everything — but now, **it must change again.** This time, we must evolve from pure digitization to **responsible digitization.** Not just fast. Not just scalable. But **sustainable**.

And that shift will not happen from boardrooms or whitepapers. It will happen when **individual architects, developers, and leaders** like us ask different questions.

Not just:

- "How quickly can this run?"

But also:

- "How responsibly can this scale?"

We are not just system builders anymore.

We are **impact designers.**

And it's time we built a digital world that doesn't just perform — but **preserves**.

⇥⇥⇥⇥⇥⇥⇥

WHAT IS SUSTAINABILITY ARCHITECTURE?

Designing Systems That Respect the Planet

Chapter 3

What Is Sustainability Architecture?

"Designing Systems That Respect the Planet"

In my early years as a Digital Architect, I believed that success meant fast systems, clean UIs, and business value delivered on time. I took pride in automation, uptime, and reducing human intervention.

But over time, a deeper question emerged in my work:

It's a question few digital professionals stop to ask. Because sustainability, for years, was treated as someone else's problem — a separate team, a separate goal, a separate report. But I realized something simple, yet profound:

"Every digital decision is also a climate decision."
— Satya Prakash (© 2025)

That's when I began shaping my role not just around architecture — but **Sustainability Architecture.**

🧩 So, What Is Sustainability Architecture?

It's not just about using renewable energy or shutting off idle servers. It's about designing systems — from the ground up — that are efficient, transparent, adaptive, and built with **ecological and ethical intelligence.**

Think of it as **embedding environmental responsibility into enterprise IT strategy.**

It means asking:

- Can this system consume less energy?
- Can this process eliminate waste?
- Can the data we collect be used to track carbon emissions?
- Are we designing for the full lifecycle — not just the launch?

Sustainability Architecture is **not a role**, it's a mindset — one that balances performance with preservation.

⇥⇥⇥⇥⇥⇥⇥

🏗 Core Pillars of Sustainability Architecture

1. **Energy-Aware Design**

   Every design decision — from server selection to code efficiency — affects energy usage. Choosing green cloud regions, optimizing algorithms, and reducing redundant workloads are small changes that scale to big impact.

2. **Responsible Automation**

   RPA and AI should not just replicate manual work — they should **remove unnecessary work altogether.**

True automation doesn't just shift the load — it reduces the load.

3. **Carbon Intelligence**

   By building systems that **measure and surface CO_2 data** in real-time, we enable leaders to make better decisions. Sustainability KPIs must sit beside cost and performance metrics.

4. **Lifecycle Thinking**

   Most systems are built to launch — few are built to **retire responsibly.** A sustainability architect thinks about:

   - Asset reuse
   - Software decommissioning
   - Hardware recycling
   - Energy offsets

5. **User-Centric Nudging**

   Sometimes, technology can empower behavior change. Alerts that remind users to shut down unused VMs, dashboards that visualize impact, and default eco-modes can reduce consumption without sacrificing function.

⇥⇥⇥⇥⇥⇥⇥

🔄 The Shift from "Sustainable IT" to "Sustainable Thinking"

Sustainability is not a checklist. It is a **design principle.**

And just like security became "everyone's job" in tech, sustainability must become **a shared responsibility** — across development, architecture, infrastructure, governance, and even product design.

"We're not just here to code better — we're here to code responsibly."
— Satya Prakash (© 2025)

That's what Sustainability Architecture enables — not just smarter systems, but **systems that care.**

⇥⇥⇥⇥⇥⇥⇥

🧭 Looking Ahead

In the chapters that follow, I'll walk you through how we can apply sustainability thinking across major digital domains — from energy, water, lighting, and automation to cloud operations and AI workloads.

You'll see not just principles, but **practical frameworks** — drawn from real-world architecture, enterprise transformation, and the collective goal of **building a net-zero digital world.**

We are entering a time where systems must do more than deliver — they must **respect**.

Sustainability Architecture is not just my profession. It is my purpose.

And this book is your blueprint to make it yours too.

AI Optimizing Energy Efficiency

Chapter 4

Energy Efficiency through AI

"Smarter Systems for a Cooler Planet"

The world doesn't just run on power — it runs on decisions. And today, more and more of those decisions are made by **AI**.

In boardrooms, factories, and data canters, artificial intelligence is automating operations, optimizing processes, and delivering value in real time. But what if AI could do more than predict trends or flag anomalies?

What if it could help us **conserve energy** and **protect the planet**?

🗲 Rethinking Efficiency

For years, energy efficiency meant switching to LEDs or buying ENERGY STAR-rated devices. But today, efficiency is far more dynamic — it's not just what devices you use, but **how intelligently they run**.

That's where AI enters the frame — not as a luxury, but as a **necessity**.

"The most sustainable watt is the one you never use — and the smartest system is the one that knows when not to run."
— Satya Prakash (© 2025)

AI empowers us to create digital systems that:

- Run only when needed
- Predict energy spikes before they happen
- Reduce waste across infrastructure
- Adapt to environmental conditions in real time

🏢 A Real-World Parallel

In one of the global projects I supported, the organization had thousands of virtual machines (VMs) running across multiple regions. Most were left idle after office hours, consuming compute, cooling, and carbon.

We deployed a simple AI-powered monitoring tool that used predictive models to detect usage patterns and suggest auto-shutdown schedules. The result? Over **30% reduction** in idle energy use within the first 90 days.

Not a single user noticed any change in performance. But the planet certainly did.

That's the power of intelligent efficiency.

🧠 Where AI Makes the Difference

1. **Dynamic Load Balancing**

   AI can redistribute workloads based on server efficiency, time of day, or real-time energy pricing — reducing both emissions and operating costs.

2. **Predictive Cooling in Data Centers**

   Instead of maintaining fixed cooling thresholds, AI models adapt to environmental data and server load, keeping temperatures within optimal ranges using **less energy**.

3. **Smart Scheduling**

   Machine learning models can analyze peak vs. off-peak usage and automatically defer non-critical jobs to greener windows — when renewable energy availability is higher or demand is lower.

4. **Anomaly Detection**

   AI can flag abnormal energy consumption across devices, processes, or departments — sometimes even before humans notice the spike.

But What About AI's Own Footprint?

It's a fair question — and one I welcome:

"Isn't AI itself harmful to the environment? Doesn't it run on massive, power-hungry data centers?"

The answer is **yes — if misused.**

But **no — when designed intentionally for sustainability**.

AI can be resource-intensive, especially when training **large-scale, general-purpose models** like those used in open-ended language generation. But in the context of sustainability architecture, we take a **targeted approach**.

Here's how we minimize AI's footprint:

- We use **lightweight, purpose-built models**, often trained once or infrequently

- These models are deployed on **existing infrastructure**, not scaled in isolation
- Their job is to **reduce energy waste**, not add to it
- We measure the **Carbon ROI** — ensuring the emissions saved far outweigh the emissions spent

"AI isn't automatically sustainable. But applied thoughtfully, it becomes one of our most powerful tools for decarbonization."
— Satya Prakash (© 2025)

Think of it like using a drone to locate forest fires early. Yes, the drone consumes battery — but the fire it prevents saves hectares of forest. The same principle applies here: the **right use of AI** enables proactive energy management, real-time optimization, and intelligent shutdown — all of which help shrink digital carbon footprints.

→I→I→I→I→I→I→I

🌱 From Reactive to Proactive

Traditional IT systems are **reactive**: they wait for thresholds to break before acting. AI-driven systems are **proactive**: they anticipate, adapt, and optimize in real time.

That shift — from reactive to proactive — is the core of sustainable architecture.

"Efficiency is no longer about less. It's about knowing enough to use only what's needed."
— Satya Prakash (© 2025)

→I→I→I→I→I→I→I

💡 Challenges to Overcome

Of course, deploying AI itself isn't without cost. Training large models can consume significant energy — and must be done responsibly. The key is **targeted, lightweight, domain-specific AI**, designed not to chase novelty, but to **optimize impact**.

Governance, explainability, and ethical AI frameworks must also be embedded—especially in sustainability systems where unintended consequences could affect entire facilities or ecosystems.

→|→|→|→|→|→|→|

🌍 Your Role as a Sustainability Architect

As a Sustainability Architect, your responsibility is not to just implement AI, but to **guide how AI thinks about energy**:

- Set carbon-aware objectives in AI models
- Define sustainable defaults in infrastructure-as-code
- Use AI to uncover what human analysis often misses
- Build explainable AI dashboards for energy teams

This isn't the future — it's the **now**. And we have the tools.

We no longer have to choose between intelligence and responsibility.

We can, and must, **design both** into the architecture.

→|→|→|→|→|→|→|

🔚 Final Thought

AI will continue to reshape the way we live, work, and power the world. But the real question isn't how advanced our models become. It's whether they can help us live within our means — not just financially, but **ecologically**.

Because a truly sustainable system isn't just built with AI. It's built with **awareness**.

WATER CONSERVATION

Chapter 5

Water Conservation

"Every Drop Counts — Even in Digital"

When we talk about sustainability in the digital world, we often think about electricity, emissions, and hardware waste. **Water rarely enters the conversation**.

But the truth is, **water is silently powering the digital economy**. From data centre cooling to manufacturing semiconductors, trillions of litres are used — and often wasted — to keep technology running.

As Sustainability Architects, we must remember:

"You can't build resilient systems on a planet that's running dry."
— Satya Prakash (© 2025)

This chapter explores how **natural water scarcity** teaches us to design smarter, more responsible digital systems — and why **water conservation is a central pillar** of sustainability.

💧 Nature's Signal: A Drought That Changed Everything

In 2019, a major city in South India came close to what experts called "Day Zero" — the day when taps would run dry. Dams dropped to 0.1% capacity. Tankers lined up for hours. Offices sent workers home. IT parks struggled to cool servers or flush toilets.

This wasn't fiction. It was the result of:

- Rapid urbanization
- Over-extraction of groundwater
- No early warning systems
- Lack of water-resilient infrastructure

And that's where **digital and natural systems intersect**.

The lesson?

Even the most modern cities collapse without water.

Even the most advanced servers fail if the cooling stops.

Even the best software halts when nature says "no more."

⇥⇥⇥⇥⇥⇥⇥

🧭 Why Water Conservation Matters in Sustainability

Sustainability isn't just about CO_2.

It's about **resource balance** — and water is one of the most **critical, finite** resources we have.

Water scarcity leads to:

- Food insecurity
- Energy supply disruptions
- Manufacturing delays
- Migration and social unrest
- IT infrastructure outages

Water connects all sustainability pillars:

🌿 Environment ⟶ 💼 Economy ⟶ 👥 Society ⟶ 🔌 Infrastructure

🧠 What Architects Can Learn from Nature

Nature never wastes. Every drop is recycled.

Rivers adapt their flow. Plants store water. Clouds wait for balance before release.

If nature can adapt, so can we — through:

- **Designing systems that recycle water** (closed-loop cooling, greywater reuse)
- **Using AI to detect leaks and overuse**
- Optimizing processes to reduce water-intensive operations
- Deploying infrastructure in water-abundant zones

"Nature is not just our resource — it's our blueprint."
— Satya Prakash (© 2025)

⇥⇥⇥⇥⇥⇥⇥

💡 From Natural to Digital: How Water Connects All Systems

Natural World	Digital/Enterprise Equivalent
Rivers drying up	Cooling failures in data centers
Groundwater depletion	Overuse of hidden system resources
Rainwater harvesting	Resource optimization in cloud workloads
Drought-resistant crops	Lightweight AI models built to conserve energy & water

As architects, we must **map natural logic to digital design**.

✅ Real-World Actions for Architects & Enterprises

- **Avoid building in water-scarce regions** without mitigation
- Use **IoT sensors** to monitor water in plants, data centers, and office campuses
- Choose vendors and cloud regions with **published WUE (Water Usage Effectiveness)**
- Build **resilience** into digital systems that depend on water — especially cooling and energy backup

"We don't just conserve water to save money. We conserve it to secure the future."

— Satya Prakash (© 2025)

→I→I→I→I→I→I→I

🔚 Final Thought

Every drought we ignore brings us closer to digital instability. Every drop we save adds resilience to the systems we depend on.

Sustainability isn't just about building greener.

It's about building **wiser**, with nature as a co-designer — not an afterthought.

And the first step in that wisdom is respecting water — the quiet engine behind every living and digital thing.

SUSTAINABLE LIGHTING DESIGN

Chapter 6

Sustainable Lighting Design

"Illuminating a Greener Path, One Lumen at a Time"

When people think about sustainability in architecture, they often overlook one of the most visible elements: **light**.

But lighting is everywhere — in homes, offices, factories, hospitals, roads, and server rooms. It's the first thing we switch on, and usually the last thing we think to optimize.

Yet lighting alone can account for up to **15% of global electricity consumption**, and in some sectors, it's much higher.

"If energy is the bloodstream of modern infrastructure, lighting is its pulse — steady, essential, and full of potential to change."

— Satya Prakash (© 2025)

→|→|→|→|→|→|→|

💡 The Hidden Cost of Light

Many companies have upgraded to LED and assume their job is done. But real sustainable lighting goes far beyond just swapping out bulbs.

Poorly designed lighting systems often result in:

- **Over-illumination** (lighting unused areas or during daylight)
- **Manual operation** (human forgetfulness or negligence)
- **Lack of automation** (no dimming, scheduling, or daylight sensing)
- **High CO_2 footprint** from round-the-clock lighting in smart factories, warehouses, and retail zones

As a Sustainability Architect, I've seen lighting audits reveal **up to 40% excess energy use** just from poor configuration.

Nature's Blueprint: Light with Purpose

In nature, light is never wasted.

- Trees grow toward it
- Animals rise and rest with it
- The earth rotates in harmony with the sun

"Nature doesn't light everything. It lights just enough, at the right time."

— Satya Prakash (© 2025)

This is the mindset that should guide **Sustainable Lighting Design** in digital infrastructure.

→|→|→|→|→|→|→|

🧭 Principles of Sustainable Lighting Architecture

1. **Design for Function, Not Aesthetics**

   Begin with use-cases, not looks. Bright corridors, unused storage areas, or excessive façade lighting add cost without value. Lighting should **serve function first**.

2. **Use Smart Controls**

   Integrate motion sensors, daylight sensors, timers, and smart switches to:

- Automatically turn lights off in empty spaces
- Dim lighting based on ambient light
- Schedule night-mode for exterior fixtures

3. **LED Is Just the Start**

   Choose LED fixtures with **high luminous efficacy (lm/W)** and long lifecycle, but also ensure they're **maintained properly**. Dust-covered LED panels or outdated drivers lose efficiency.

4. **Implement Zonal Lighting**

   Instead of lighting entire floors, implement **task-based or zonal lighting**. For example:

- In warehouses: only light active aisles
- In open offices: desk clusters rather than full ceilings
- In server rooms: sensor-triggered aisle lighting

5. **Cloud-Connected Lighting Analytics**

   Use IoT platforms to monitor lighting usage patterns, energy draw, and carbon impact. Some smart systems even **self-correct** based on occupancy and daylight data.

⇥⇥⇥⇥⇥⇥⇥

🏢 A Real-Life Example

At a corporate headquarters I consulted for, over 60% of the office lights were active 24/7 — including stairwells, meeting rooms, and print areas. The team assumed sensors were in place. They weren't.

By implementing a smart lighting system that used motion detection, daylight harvesting, and scheduling APIs, we achieved:

- **38% energy savings in the first year**
- Improved employee comfort
- A clear reduction in cooling loads (lights emit heat!)

⇥⇥⇥⇥⇥⇥⇥

🌍 Sustainability Impact Beyond Energy

Smart lighting doesn't just reduce electricity bills. It helps:

- **Lower HVAC load** by reducing heat from excessive lighting
- **Improve human well-being** with circadian lighting

- **Avoid nighttime light pollution** in cities

Contribute to **LEED/BREEAM sustainability certifications**

Lighting is one of the fastest ROIs in green retrofits — both financially and environmentally.

→I→I→I→I→I→I→I

🔧 Architecting for the Future

As a Sustainability Architect, your role isn't just to choose LED or reduce lumens. It's to **build lighting into the digital nervous system**:

- Integrate with building management systems (BMS)
- Align lighting use with occupancy data from IoT sensors
- Measure CO_2 savings per zone through analytics

Enable remote management through cloud automation

"When we bring intelligence to lighting, we bring light to sustainability itself."
— Satya Prakash (© 2025)

🌿 Beyond Efficiency: Can Lights Clean the Air?

Most lighting strategies focus on **using less** — less power, less heat, less pollution. But what if light could do **more than reduce harm**?

What if it could actually **heal** the environment?

This is a question I've reflected on deeply. One of my recent thoughts was:

*"Why stop at energy efficiency? Can we build lighting systems that actually **absorb CO_2** from the air?"*
— Satya Prakash (© 2025)

The idea isn't just futuristic — it›s possible.

🧪 Concepts in Development:

1. **Moss-Integrated Fixtures**

   Moss naturally captures CO_2 and particulate matter. Integrating bio-reactive moss panels into street lights or office fixtures could allow lighting units to **illuminate and purify** simultaneously.

2. **Algae-Based Lighting Structures**

   Algae consumes CO_2 for photosynthesis. Experimental prototypes already use algae tubes in light poles to reduce urban carbon and generate oxygen — a natural CO▯ sink embedded into infrastructure.

3. **Titanium Dioxide (TiO_2) Coating**

   TiO_2, when exposed to light, can trigger **photocatalytic reactions** that break down pollutants, including nitrogen oxides and VOCs. Lights coated with TiO_2 can **clean the surrounding air** under UV exposure — turning lighting into a passive air purifier

🔚 Final Thought

Sustainable lighting is not about darkness.

It's about **thoughtful, data-driven illumination**.

Every switch matters. Every sensor saves. Every lumen, when used wisely, becomes a step toward a carbon-neutral tomorrow.

Let there be light — not waste.

AUTOMATION IN SUSTAINABILITY ARCHITECTURE

Chapter 7

Automation for Resource Optimization

"Designing Systems That Think Before They Consume"

Automation is often discussed in terms of productivity. Less manual effort. More speed. Lower cost.

But in the age of climate crisis, automation's real value lies in something deeper:

> *"The most sustainable system is not just one that works without people — but one that works without wasting."*
> — *Satya Prakash (© 2025)*

When automation is embedded into the digital architecture with sustainability in mind, it transforms into a powerful engine for **resource conservation** — saving **energy**, **water**, **materials**, and **emissions**.

🔄 From Process Automation to Purpose Automation

Traditional automation focuses on replacing human tasks.

Sustainable automation focuses on **optimizing system behavior** — not just to get things done, but to do them **better** and **greener**.

Examples:

- Shutting down idle infrastructure automatically
- Adjusting lighting and HVAC in real-time
- Scheduling compute jobs during renewable energy windows
- Reducing water flow based on sensor data
- Auto-calibrating machines to reduce material waste

⇥⇥⇥⇥⇥⇥⇥

🏢 Real-World Example: Manufacturing Plant Automation

At one advanced manufacturing facility I evaluated, robotic arms, conveyors, and laser cutters were running 24/7 — even when no production was scheduled for certain shifts.

By applying IoT automation and AI scheduling logic, we were able to:

- Automatically power down unused zones
- Trigger standby mode based on operator absence
- Sync processes to demand-based production cycles

The result:

- ✓ 23% reduction in electricity use
- ✓ 18% drop in machine wear-and-tear
- ✓ 2.1 metric tons less CO□ per month

And the best part? No loss in output.

"Automation should make things faster, yes — but more importantly, it should make them wiser."
— Satya Prakash (© 2025)

🧠 Where Automation Makes the Most Impact

1. **Energy Optimization**

   Smart meters + automation = peak load shedding, idle shutdowns, and time-based optimization without human intervention.

2. **Building Management Systems (BMS)**

   Lighting, HVAC, ventilation, and blinds—all orchestrated by smart rules based on occupancy, time, and weather — drastically cut energy waste.

3. **Water Use Monitoring**

   IoT valves, sensors, and controllers automatically reduce water pressure, detect leaks, or recycle greywater based on usage patterns.

4. **Material Flow in Warehouses**

   RFID tags and automated conveyors can reduce overproduction, packaging waste, and even optimize shipping routes.

5. **Cloud & Data Workloads**

   Automation scripts can spin down unused servers, reassign VMs, and shift jobs to off-peak renewable-powered hours — reducing digital carbon.

→I→I→I→I→I→I→I

🌿 Automation as a Sustainability Multiplier

Automation doesn't replace sustainability efforts — it **amplifies them**.

Instead of asking humans to remember to save — automation **makes saving the default behavior**.

- In this way, automation becomes:
- A thermostat for energy
- A faucet for water
- A gatekeeper for materials
- A watchdog for emissions

"Well-designed automation isn't just efficient. It's ethical."
— Satya Prakash (© 2025)

🧭 Framework: R.O.A.D. to Sustainable Automation

Here's a 4-step strategy I use when embedding automation into sustainability architecture:

- **R – Recognize**: Identify resource-intensive processes
- **O – Optimize**: Streamline for minimum waste
- **A – Automate**: Apply logic to remove human error
- **D – Decarbonize**: Quantify impact and align to CO goals

This framework ensures automation is not just functional — but meaningful.

→I→I→I→I→I→I→I

🛑 Pitfalls to Avoid

- **Over-automation**: Too much automation can lead to complexity and rebound effects (e.g., more machines = more emissions)
- **Lack of monitoring**: Unchecked systems may operate inefficiently over time
- **Ignoring lifecycle emissions**: Automation hardware (sensors, actuators) has its own footprint — it must be justified by long-term gains

🔚 Final Thought

Automation, when used with wisdom and intent, becomes more than just a tool for efficiency — it becomes a **guardian of resources**.

In a world that can no longer afford waste, automation is not about doing more.

It's about doing **just enough — at the right time, with the least impact**.

CLOUD
SUSTAINABILITY
STRATEGY

Chapter 8

Cloud Sustainability Strategy

"Designing a Cleaner Sky in the Cloud"

The cloud was once seen only as a tool for scalability and cost savings.

Today, it's increasingly viewed through a new lens:

Can the cloud be sustainable?

"The future of IT won't just be faster or cheaper — it must be cleaner."

— Satya Prakash (© 2025)

As workloads migrate to public, private, and hybrid cloud platforms, enterprises face a new challenge: **how to ensure that this digital shift doesn't come with a hidden environmental cost.**

This is where the **Cloud Sustainability Strategy** becomes vital.

→|→|→|→|→|→|→|

☁ Why the Cloud Matters for Sustainability

Cloud computing contributes to carbon emissions in three key ways:

- **Data** center energy use
- **Cooling systems and water consumption**
- **Hardware lifecycle and e-waste**

While hyperscale providers often use energy-efficient designs, your sustainability impact depends on **what, where, and how** you deploy in the cloud.

💡 Real-World Insight: Region Matters

While advising a client during a multi-region cloud rollout, we compared two seemingly identical zones — both offered by the same cloud provider, same price, same specs.

But their **carbon intensities** were radically different:

- **Region A**: powered 80% by renewable sources
- **Region B**: powered 65% by coal and thermal plants

By shifting 60% of workloads to Region A, we reduced their indirect emissions by over **22 metric tons of CO_2 annually**, with **no impact on performance**.

"In the cloud, every location has a footprint. Architect with your eyes open."
— Satya Prakash (© 2025)

→|→|→|→|→|→|→|

🧠 Principles of a Cloud Sustainability Strategy

1. **Select Green Regions**

   Every cloud provider publishes **Carbon Intensity by Region**. Use this to:

- Choose greener zones for non-latency-sensitive workloads
- Avoid water-scarce regions for water-cooled data centers
- Plan disaster recovery with sustainability in mind, not just geography

2. **Right-Size Everything**

   Avoid over-provisioning. Scale compute, storage, and bandwidth based on real usage.

- Use serverless, auto-scaling, and ephemeral services
- Decommission idle VMs and containers
- Schedule batch jobs during renewable-heavy energy windows

3. **Use Cloud-Native Sustainability Tools**

   Most major cloud providers offer:

- CO_2 dashboards
- Energy efficiency reports

- API-based emissions estimators These tools should be integrated into cloud governance and FinOps.

4. Sustainable Code & Architecture

Lightweight apps and optimized APIs consume less cloud power:

- Reduce API polling and unnecessary I/O
- Use content delivery networks (CDNs) to lower latency and energy
- Archive cold data — don't keep everything "hot"

→I→I→I→I→I→I→I

🧭 Framework: The 5P Model for Cloud Sustainability

I use a strategic framework called **5P** when evaluating cloud designs for environmental impact:

Pillar	Description
Provider	Choose vendors with clean energy and transparency
Platform	Favor serverless, PaaS, or managed services
Placement	Select regions with low carbon and water stress
Performance	Optimize for efficiency, not just speed
Policy	Set governance for decommissioning and measurement

"Great cloud design doesn't just move fast. It moves smart — and sustainable."
— Satya Prakash (© 2025)

→I→I→I→I→I→I→I

💼 Benefits Beyond the Environment

Cloud sustainability is not just about the planet.

It also delivers:

- Lower operating costs
- Longer infrastructure life
- Regulatory and ESG alignment
- Increased investor confidence
- Support for net-zero enterprise goals

→I→I→I→I→I→I→I

⚠ Pitfalls to Avoid

- **Cloud sprawl**: Unmonitored growth leads to excessive compute and carbon
- **Ignoring embodied carbon**: Sustainability isn't only about runtime — it's also about manufacturing emissions
- **Greenwashing risk**: Relying solely on provider PR, not verifiable data

→I→I→I→I→I→I→I

🔗 Sustainable Procurement in the Cloud Era

As organizations shift to Software-as-a-Service (SaaS) models, much of their carbon footprint and resource impact is **outsourced** — but not **eliminated**.

That's why **vendor selection** now plays a critical role in cloud sustainability.

"When you choose a SaaS vendor, you're not just buying a product — you're buying into their values, data center practices, and carbon impact."

— Satya Prakash (© 2025)

A sustainable procurement strategy should ensure that your **third-party cloud partners** uphold the same environmental standards you apply internally.

→|→|→|→|→|→|→|

✅ Key Criteria for Evaluating Sustainable SaaS Vendors

Here's what a Sustainability Architect should look for when choosing or renewing a SaaS vendor:

1. **Green Hosting**

- Does the vendor host on a cloud platform powered by renewable energy?
- Do they disclose regional carbon intensity?
- Are they certified (e.g., LEED, ISO 14001)?

2. **Transparent Emissions Reporting**

- Does the vendor publish an annual **GHG inventory**, particularly Scope 2 (energy used) and Scope 3 (supply chain)?
- Are CO□ savings from SaaS usage benchmarked?

3. **Software Efficiency**

- Does the application scale efficiently based on user load?
- Does it support data archiving, edge delivery, or low-power modes?
- Is it optimized to reduce bandwidth, compute, and storage?

4. **Data Residency & Regional Placement**

- Can the customer choose **low-carbon regions** for data hosting?
- Is multi-region replication optional or forced?

5. **Sustainable Procurement Policy**

- Is the vendor actively decarbonizing their own procurement, hardware, and cloud usage?
- Are environmental and social criteria applied to their suppliers?

"Your vendor's footprint becomes your footprint — choose wisely."

— Satya Prakash (© 2025)

Framework: The S.A.A.S. Vendor Checklist

I often use the **S.A.A.S.** framework when evaluating SaaS platforms from a sustainability standpoint:

S	**Source: Where is the solution hosted, and what is the cloud region's carbon intensity?**
A	**Architecture:** Is the software optimized for minimal compute, storage, and transfer?
A	**Accountability:** Does the vendor report emissions and follow verified environmental metrics?
S	**Sustainability Alignment:** Do they have public commitments to net-zero or ESG alignment?

Practical Example

One finance company I supported was using five different SaaS tools across HR, billing, collaboration, and analytics.

After performing a **sustainability audit** across vendors, we discovered:

- 2 vendors had no green energy policy
- 1 stored data in high-carbon intensity zones
- Only 1 provided CO_2 emissions reporting per customer

Using the S.A.A.S. framework, they consolidated tools and switched to vendors that offered:

✓ Renewable-powered hosting

✓ Carbon metrics APIs

✓ Sustainability certifications

The result? A **12.6% reduction in digital emissions** without compromising functionality.

🔚 Final Note on Procurement

You cannot build a sustainable digital future with unsustainable partners.

Whether it's a core cloud provider, a small SaaS vendor, or an AI model API — every procurement decision is also a **carbon decision**.

"Sustainability is not a checkbox in vendor onboarding — it's the gatekeeper of long-term value."
— Satya Prakash (© 2025)

🔚 Final Thought

The cloud is not magic — it's physical.

Every API call, every VM, every database query draws energy, emits heat, and depends on natural resources.

Your architecture choices in the cloud ripple outward — into the power grid, the water table, and the global atmosphere.

"You may not own the cloud's infrastructure, but you do own its impact."
— Satya Prakash (© 2025)

Cloud sustainability is no longer optional. It is the foundation of resilient, ethical, and future-ready digital architecture

CIRCULAR ECONOMY AND DIGITAL TWINS

Chapter 9

Circular Economy and Digital Twins

"Building Systems That Reuse, Regenerate, and Rethink"

In nature, nothing is wasted. Fallen leaves become compost. Water evaporates and returns as rain. Life follows a closed-loop system — the original circular economy.

Digital architecture, however, has long relied on a **linear model**: extract resources → build → consume → discard.

But this model is no longer viable.

As natural resources deplete and e-waste surges, the future belongs to **circular systems** — and **Digital Twins** are emerging as a core enabler of this transformation.

"Circularity is no longer an option — it is a requirement for long-term digital survival."
— Satya Prakash (© 2025)

♻ What Is the Circular Economy?

A circular economy is based on three principles:

1. Design out waste and pollution
2. Keep products and materials in use
3. Regenerate natural systems

In the digital world, this means:

- **Reusing infrastructure** instead of constantly replacing it
- **Refurbishing and redeploying devices**
- **Designing systems for repairability and resilience**
- **Recovering data and energy** through feedback and optimization

Circular IT applies this mindset to hardware, software, and system design.

🧠 What Are Digital Twins?

A **Digital Twin** is a real-time, virtual replica of a physical object, process, or system. It continuously receives data from sensors and IoT devices, allowing architects and engineers to **monitor, simulate, and optimize performance**.

In sustainability architecture, Digital Twins serve two purposes:

- **Minimize resource consumption** by simulating better behavior
- **Extend lifecycle** through predictive maintenance and intelligent decisions

🔄 Where Digital Twins Support Circularity

1. **Manufacturing**

   A Digital Twin of a factory can:

- Track material use in real-time
- Predict breakdowns and reduce equipment replacement
- Optimize energy, water, and waste processes

2. **Smart Buildings**

   A twin of a building monitors lighting, HVAC, occupancy, and energy to:

- Prolong the life of systems
- Trigger automated maintenance
- Minimize environmental impact over the building's lifespan

3. **Urban Infrastructure**

   City planners use digital twins to:

- Model traffic flows and reduce emissions
- Manage utilities like water reuse or waste segregation
- Monitor public assets for circular maintenance

🌍 Real-World Example: Data Center Circularity

A European cloud provider created a Digital Twin of its data center to:

- Predict server overheating
- Automate cooling adjustments
- Trigger hardware rotation before failure
- Reuse old machines in non-critical workloads

This approach extended hardware life by 28% and reduced e-waste by 34 metric tons annually.

"When you can see how your system breathes, you can teach it to breathe cleaner."
— Satya Prakash (© 2025)

🧭 Framework: The D.I.G.I.T. Model for Circular Tech with Twins

D – Design for Circularity	**Start with modular, repairable, upgradable systems**
I – Integrate Real-Time Data	Connect sensors and IoT devices to monitor usage
G – Generate Insights with Twins	Use simulation to forecast failure, waste, or inefficiency
I – Implement Adaptive Controls	Trigger automation based on twin predictions
T – Track Lifecycle Impacts	Measure CO_2 savings, lifespan extension, and reuse outcomes

→|→|→|→|→|→|→|

♻ Circular Design Thinking for Digital Products

Even software should follow circular principles:

- Write **efficient, modular code** that can be reused and updated
- Avoid unnecessary compute and storage consumption

- Use **open standards** and APIs to extend software longevity
- Build platforms that support **multi-device compatibility**

The less you replace, the more you preserve.

→|→|→|→|→|→|→|

⚠ Pitfalls to Avoid

- Treating digital twins as static models rather than real-time systems
- Using twins only for performance, not sustainability
- Failing to measure lifecycle emissions or embodied carbon in IT purchases

→|→|→|→|→|→|→|

🔚 Final Thought

Digital Twins give us **eyes and intelligence** into our systems. The circular economy gives us the **purpose and ethics** to use that vision wisely.

Together, they offer a powerful blueprint for **regenerative digital architecture**.

"A circular economy doesn't just reduce waste. It restores balance."
— Satya Prakash (© 2025)

Let us build systems that know when to pause, reuse, repair, and regenerate.

Because true sustainability isn't just smart — it's cyclical.

AI
HVAC OPTIMIZATION
WITH AI
MAKING BUILDINGS BREATHE SMARTER

Chapter 10

HVAC Optimization with AI

"Making Buildings Breathe Smarter"

Heating, Ventilation, and Air Conditioning (HVAC) systems are essential to building comfort — but they are also one of the **biggest contributors to energy consumption** and **operational carbon emissions** in commercial and industrial infrastructure.

Globally, HVAC systems account for nearly **40% of a building's energy use**, making them a primary target for sustainability-focused transformation.

"If energy is the bloodstream of a building, HVAC is its heartbeat. And AI is how we make that heartbeat smarter."
— Satya Prakash (© 2025)

🌡 The Energy Challenge

Most HVAC systems operate on fixed schedules or outdated sensors, leading to:

- Overcooling or overheating in unused zones
- Inconsistent airflow distribution
- Delayed response to real-time conditions
- High energy and maintenance costs

These inefficiencies create not only financial losses but also environmental ones — especially in **climate-controlled buildings**, such as hospitals, data centers, and offices.

→|→|→|→|→|→|→|

🤖 How AI Optimizes HVAC

By integrating Artificial Intelligence into HVAC systems, buildings can:

- **Predict demand** using occupancy, weather, and usage patterns
- **Automate control** for chillers, vents, and thermostats
- **Reduce load peaks** and adjust in real-time
- **Detect anomalies** in equipment and prevent energy waste

This results in more consistent temperatures, lower energy bills, reduced CO_2 output, and longer equipment lifespan.

→|→|→|→|→|→|→|

💼 Real-World Example: Smart Campus HVAC

A multinational IT firm implemented AI-driven HVAC across its 5-building campus:

- Sensors tracked occupancy, weather, CO_2 levels, and humidity
- AI algorithms adjusted airflow and cooling zones every 5 minutes
- Predictive analytics flagged malfunctioning dampers before breakdown

Impact in Year 1:

✓ 31% energy savings on HVAC

✓ 490 metric tons of CO_2 emissions avoided

✓ 20% increase in system uptime

→|→|→|→|→|→|→|

🧠 Components of AI-Enabled HVAC Architecture

Layer	Function
Sensors & IoT	Collect real-time data on temperature, humidity, occupancy, and CO_2
Edge Processing	Local AI analysis near equipment for faster control decisions
Cloud AI Models	Forecast cooling/heating needs, detect patterns, optimize schedules
Integration Layer	Connects with BMS (Building Management System) and energy dashboards
User Interface	Visualizes performance, emissions, and recommendations

🧭 Framework: The A.I.R. Model for HVAC Optimization

A – Analyze Patterns	**Use historical and live data to predict HVAC demand**
I – Intelligent Control	Enable real-time adjustments based on usage, weather, and occupancy
R – Reduce Emissions	Quantify and lower CO□ output through automation and efficiency

"Sustainable HVAC is not just about airflow — it's about insight flow."

— Satya Prakash (© 2025)

⇥⇥⇥⇥⇥⇥⇥

⚠ Common Pitfalls

- **Neglecting sensor calibration**, leading to inaccurate predictions
- **Over-reliance on cloud-only AI**, causing latency in control
- **No integration with renewable sources**, missing full optimization
- **Ignoring occupant feedback**, risking comfort and adoption

⇥⇥⇥⇥⇥⇥⇥

🔗 Integration with Other Systems

AI-optimized HVAC systems can also:

- Sync with **smart lighting** to adjust based on daylight and temperature synergy
- Interface with **renewable energy systems** (e.g., solar) to time energy usage
- Feed into **digital twins** for predictive maintenance and long-term modeling

🔚 Final Thought

HVAC is no longer just a mechanical system — it's a data-driven, intelligent network that can either consume or conserve, depending on how it's architected.

By infusing AI into this critical infrastructure layer, we ensure buildings are not just efficient, but **adaptive and sustainable**.

Chapter 11

Smart Buildings and IoT

"Architecting Intelligent Spaces for Sustainable Living"

Modern buildings are evolving from passive infrastructure into intelligent ecosystems — capable of sensing, learning, and optimizing themselves in real-time. At the heart of this transformation lies the fusion of **Internet of Things (IoT)** technologies and **smart systems**.

Smart buildings are no longer a futuristic concept; they are a **core pillar of sustainable architecture**.

"A building that listens, learns, and adapts is not just smart — it's sustainable."
— Satya Prakash (© 2025)

🏢 What Makes a Building 'Smart'?

A **smart building** is one that uses **interconnected sensors, devices, and data platforms** to automatically monitor and control its systems — from lighting and HVAC to water, security, and waste.

Core functions include:

- Energy optimization
- Predictive maintenance
- Occupant comfort and health tracking
- Automated system integration
- Data-driven decision-making

⇥⇥⇥⇥⇥⇥⇥

🌐 Role of IoT in Sustainable Smart Buildings

IoT enables **real-time sensing** and **automated response** to a building's conditions. Each sensor acts as a nerve in a digital nervous system — providing continuous input on how to optimize resource use.

Key IoT elements include:

- Temperature, humidity, and air quality sensors
- Motion detectors and smart lighting systems
- Occupancy and footfall sensors
- Smart water meters and leak detectors
- Connected elevators and security systems

⇥⇥⇥⇥⇥⇥⇥

🧠 Real-World Example: Green Office Transformation

A mid-sized tech park in Bangalore upgraded its legacy systems with IoT-driven smart building controls. They integrated:

- Motion-sensing LED lighting
- AI-controlled HVAC with predictive models
- Water metering with leak alerts
- Energy dashboards linked to rooftop solar panels

Results after 12 months:

✓ 36% reduction in energy use

✓ 19% decrease in water consumption

✓ Enhanced workplace satisfaction scores by 27%

⇥⇥⇥⇥⇥⇥⇥

🧭 Framework: The S.M.A.R.T. Building Model

S – Sense	**Deploy sensors to monitor real-time environment and usage**
M – Monitor	Use dashboards and AI to observe building performance
A – Automate	Trigger systems to adjust lighting, temperature, airflow
R – Reduce	Minimize waste in energy, water, and space through automation
T – Tune	Continuously optimize and reprogram systems based on feedback

"If a building can think, it should also conserve."

— *Satya Prakash (© 2025)*

📊 Benefits of Smart Sustainable Buildings

Benefit	Impact
Energy savings	Up to 30–50% reduction through automation
Carbon reduction	Lower Scope 1 and 2 emissions from building operations
Improved occupant wellbeing	Monitors air quality, light, and noise for human comfort
Predictive maintenance	Reduces downtime and asset failure
ESG reporting and compliance	Easier tracking of resource and sustainability metrics

🔗 Integration with Broader Sustainability Goals

Smart buildings also connect with:

- **Renewable energy sources** (like solar and battery storage)
- **Smart grids** to optimize when and how power is consumed
- **Circular IT** to monitor hardware health and reduce e-waste
- **Digital twins** for lifecycle modeling and sustainability planning

⇥⇥⇥⇥⇥⇥⇥

⚠ Challenges to Watch

- Privacy concerns with sensor data
- Lack of interoperability between systems
- High upfront costs without long-term planning
- Poorly configured automation leading to overcorrections

→|→|→|→|→|→|→|

🔚 Final Thought

The future of sustainable architecture will not just be built — it will be coded, connected, and constantly improving.

Smart buildings powered by IoT are not only efficient; they are **responsive**, **intuitive**, and aligned with the rhythm of human and environmental needs.

Transportation and Green Mobility

Chapter 12

Transportation and Green Mobility

"Re-Engineering How the World Moves"

Transportation is the **lifeline of global economies**, but it is also one of the largest contributors to greenhouse gas emissions — accounting for over **24% of direct CO_2 emissions** from fuel combustion worldwide.

As urban populations grow and supply chains expand, the need for **sustainable mobility solutions** becomes urgent. It's time to rethink how people, goods, and systems move — not just efficiently, but **intelligently and responsibly**.

"Mobility is not just about speed. It's about impact — and what we leave behind in motion."
— Satya Prakash (© 2025)

🚗 The Problem with Traditional Transportation

Conventional transport systems rely heavily on:

- Fossil-fuel-based vehicles
- Congested urban planning
- Inefficient route management
- Lack of real-time coordination across systems

These factors lead to:

- Increased emissions
- Air and noise pollution
- Traffic congestion
- Resource inefficiency

→I→I→I→I→I→I→I

🌱 What Is Green Mobility?

Green Mobility focuses on enabling low-emission, accessible, and efficient transport systems. It includes:

- **Electrified transport** (EVs, e-buses, e-bikes)
- **Public and shared transport models**
- **Multi-modal integration** (bike + train + ride-share)
- **Active mobility** (walking, cycling)
- **Data-driven logistics** for freight optimization

→I→I→I→I→I→I→I

🧠 The Role of AI and IoT in Sustainable Transport

Technology enables smarter and greener mobility through:

- **AI-powered traffic optimization**
- **Predictive maintenance** of electric vehicles
- **Dynamic routing** for logistics and public transit
- **IoT sensors** for monitoring emissions, wear-and-tear, and safety
- **Digital twins** of transportation networks

⇥⇥⇥⇥⇥⇥⇥

🚦 Real-World Example: AI-Powered Traffic in Pune

The Pune Smart City project deployed AI-driven traffic systems that:

- Used real-time camera data and IoT sensors
- Optimized signal timing based on congestion
- Suggested eco-routes via a public mobile app

Results after 9 months:

✓ 22% reduction in traffic delays

✓ 14% drop in fuel consumption

✓ Increased public transport adoption

⇥⇥⇥⇥⇥⇥⇥

🧭 Framework: The M.O.V.E. Model for Sustainable Mobility

M – Monitor Usage	Use data to track travel patterns, emissions, and congestion
O – Optimize Routing	Enable AI-based pathfinding and multi-modal trip planning
V – Vehicle Electrification	Shift fleets to EVs, hybrids, or hydrogen-powered alternatives
E – Enable Access	Design inclusive, affordable, and shared mobility systems

"If your journey reduces someone else's burden — that's sustainable transport."

— Satya Prakash (© 2025)

→|→|→|→|→|→|→|

📦 Greening Logistics and Supply Chains

- **Telematics**: Real-time fleet tracking for energy efficiency
- **EV fleets for last-mile delivery**: Lower urban noise and emissions
- **Warehouse proximity models**: Reduce transportation distances
- **Sustainable procurement**: Choose carriers with emissions disclosure

→|→|→|→|→|→|→|

🚲 Urban Mobility Reimagined

Cities are now investing in:

- Dedicated **bike and pedestrian lanes**
- Smart **bus rapid transit (BRT)** corridors
- **Mobility-as-a-Service (MaaS)** platforms that combine booking and payment across transport modes
- **Vehicle-to-infrastructure (V2I)** communication for real-time coordination

⇥⇥⇥⇥⇥⇥⇥

⚠ Pitfalls to Avoid

- Focusing only on electrification, not full system efficiency
- Underestimating infrastructure needs (charging, data connectivity)
- Neglecting rural mobility equity
- Ignoring the lifecycle emissions of EV battery production

⇥⇥⇥⇥⇥⇥⇥

🔚 Final Thought

Green mobility is about more than vehicles—it's about designing systems that move people and products **with purpose and efficiency**, while minimizing harm to the planet.

"True progress is when every journey takes us closer to zero."
— Satya Prakash (© 2025)

Let us build cities, fleets, and networks that don't just transport — they **transform**.

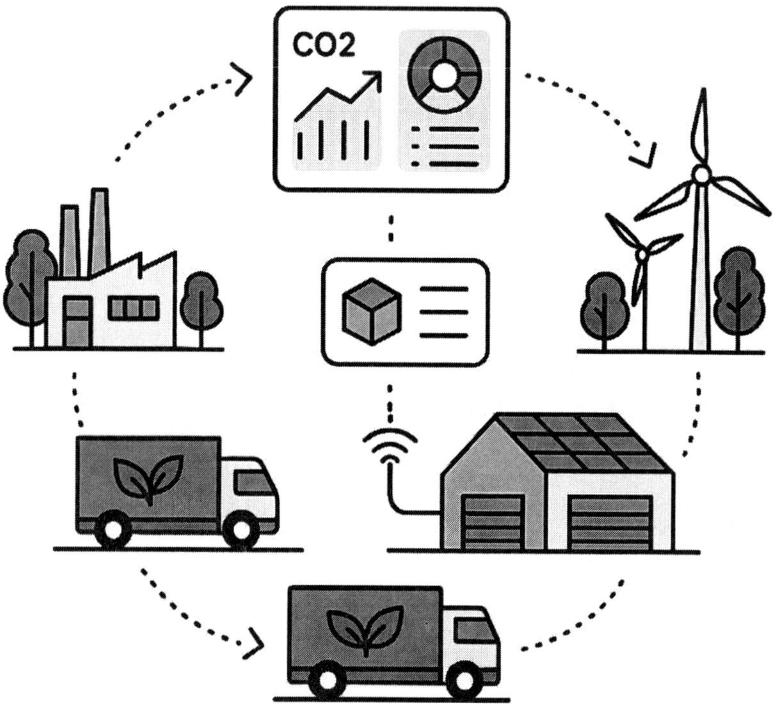
CO2

Chapter 13

Sustainable Supply Chains

"Building Ethical, Transparent, and Low-Carbon Value Networks"

Supply chains form the **invisible backbone** of the global economy — powering industries, services, and infrastructure. But they are also **responsible for more than 80% of many organizations' total carbon footprint** (Scope 3 emissions), making them a **critical focal point in sustainability transformation**.

As businesses face rising pressure from regulators, investors, and conscious consumers, the demand for **green, traceable, and resilient supply chains** is no longer optional — it's existential.

"A sustainable business doesn't just optimize the product. It reimagines the path it travels."
— Satya Prakash (© 2025)

→|→|→|→|→|→|→|

🛠 What Makes a Supply Chain Sustainable?

A **sustainable supply chain**:

- Reduces carbon emissions and resource consumption
- Promotes fair labor, safety, and ethical sourcing
- Minimizes waste across procurement, packaging, and distribution
- Is transparent, traceable, and accountable
- Embraces circularity, reuse, and low-impact logistics

⇥⇥⇥⇥⇥⇥⇥

🌍 The Global Challenge

Today's supply chains are:

- **Complex** — stretching across continents and hundreds of vendors
- **Opaque** — making emissions tracking and ESG compliance difficult
- **Resource-intensive** — with high energy, water, and waste usage
- **Vulnerable** — to geopolitical risks, climate events, and regulatory shifts

Digitization and AI offer new tools to solve these legacy challenges.

⇥⇥⇥⇥⇥⇥⇥

🧠 Role of Digital Architecture and AI

Modern sustainability architecture empowers supply chains through:

- **Digital twins of logistics**: Simulate and optimize transport, warehousing, and distribution
- **Blockchain for traceability**: Immutable records of sourcing and ESG metrics
- **AI for demand forecasting**: Prevent overproduction and reduce inventory waste
- **IoT for real-time tracking**: Monitor temperature, emissions, location, and delays
- **Sustainability dashboards**: Combine vendor, transport, and carbon data for reporting

⇥⇥⇥⇥⇥⇥⇥

📦 Real-World Example: Sustainable Procurement in Electronics

A global electronics firm transitioned from traditional to **green procurement** practices:

- Selected suppliers with carbon disclosure programs
- Audited packaging waste and shifted to recycled materials
- Used digital scorecards to assess ESG risk
- Applied AI to optimize container space and reduce air freight usage

Results after 2 years:

✓ Reduced Scope 3 emissions by 18%

✓ Saved over ₹12 crore in logistics costs

✓ Gained Tier 1 sustainability certification and investor preference

→I→I→I→I→I→I→I

🧭 Framework: The T.R.A.C.E. Model for Sustainable Supply Chains

T – Transparency	**Require full lifecycle and ESG disclosures from all vendors**
R – Responsibility	Ensure fair labor, compliance, and ethical material sourcing
A – Automation	Use AI, IoT, and RPA to optimize operations and reduce inefficiencies
C – Carbon Monitoring	Measure and reduce emissions across every node of the chain
E – Ecosystem Thinking	Collaborate with partners for mutual environmental impact reduction

"Your supply chain is a reflection of your values — automated, measured, and multiplied."

— Satya Prakash (© 2025)

→I→I→I→I→I→I→I

📊 Key Metrics to Track

Metric	Why It Matters
Scope 3 CO_2 emissions	Measures indirect impact from vendors, logistics, and use
Recyclable packaging %	Shows commitment to waste reduction and circular design
Green supplier ratio	Tracks vendors aligned with sustainability policies
Transportation emissions per kg	Measures logistics efficiency in carbon terms

🔗 Integration with Broader Architecture

Sustainable supply chain data can feed:

- **Carbon accounting platforms**
- **ESG reporting systems**
- **ERP and procurement automation tools**
- **Risk modeling engines** (for geopolitical or climate resilience)

The more connected your systems, the more measurable and actionable your sustainability efforts become.

⚠ Pitfalls to Avoid

- Choosing low-cost vendors without ESG screening
- Failing to align sustainability goals across supplier tiers
- Ignoring packaging and end-of-life impacts
- Not embedding digital traceability early in procurement architecture

🔚 Final Thought

Supply chains are not just channels for goods — they are **amplifiers of your sustainability impact**. Every node, every transaction, every kilometer adds up.

The future belongs to organizations that **don't just move fast, but move responsibly**.

Climate Resilience with
Predictive Analytics

Chapter 14

Climate Resilience with Predictive Analytics

"Preparedness is the new sustainability. In a changing climate, resilience is not a choice — it's a strategy."

Introduction

As climate-related disruptions intensify — from floods and droughts to wildfires and extreme heat — businesses and governments face growing risks to their operations, assets, and communities. These events are no longer outliers; they are becoming part of a new climate normal.

Climate resilience is the ability of a system to anticipate, absorb, adapt to, and recover from climate-related shocks. In the digital age, building this resilience demands more than reactive response — it requires predictive, data-driven strategies.

This is where **predictive analytics powered by AI and automation** steps in.

Understanding Predictive Analytics in the Climate Context
Predictive analytics uses machine learning, historical climate data, sensor input, satellite imagery, and environmental models to **forecast and simulate** future risks. These insights help organizations:

- Prepare infrastructure for heatwaves or floods
- Re-route supply chains before disruption
- Manage energy and water demand during extreme conditions
- Reduce emissions by optimizing preventive actions

🔍 Real-Life Example: Drought Prediction in Agriculture Supply Chain

Imagine a multinational food processing company that sources wheat from three major agricultural regions. With rising drought frequency due to climate change, the company faces unpredictable yields and volatile prices.

By integrating **predictive analytics**, the company:

- Uses **satellite and soil data** to predict drought 3–6 months in advance
- Combines this with **machine learning** models trained on past crop failures
- Adjusts procurement strategy by sourcing from alternate regions
- Notifies logistics partners in advance using automated alerts
- Simulates **financial risk impact** on revenue through digital twin models

As a result, the company **reduces carbon impact**, avoids last-minute air freight emissions, and ensures continuity in its supply chain — all while building climate resilience.

→I→I→I→I→I→I→I

Key Technologies in Climate Resilience Analytics

Technology	Role in Resilience
IoT Sensors	Monitor temperature, humidity, water levels in real time
Satellite Data	Assess vegetation, drought conditions, urban heat islands
Digital Twins	Simulate environmental stress on assets, buildings, crops
AI/ML Forecasting	Predict rainfall patterns, floods, wildfires
Edge Computing	Enable fast, local analysis for immediate action
Geospatial Intelligence	Map risk zones and climate vulnerability across regions

Automation and Early-Warning Systems

AI-driven systems can automatically trigger actions based on climate predictions. For instance:

- **Energy utilities** can reduce grid load before extreme heat to prevent blackouts
- **Cities** can activate drainage infrastructure in anticipation of heavy rainfall
- **Businesses** can reroute logistics before wildfires disrupt transportation

These actions are not only operational — they are climate-saving. Every rerouted shipment or prevented failure avoids CO_2 emissions and resource wastage.

KPIs for Climate Resilience through Digital Tools

KPI	What It Measures
% Accuracy of Climate Risk Forecasts	Effectiveness of ML models over time
Response Time to Climate Alerts	Agility of decision-making systems
Reduction in Supply Chain Emissions	Emission avoided due to early intervention
Asset Downtime Due to Climate Events	Resilience level of infrastructure
Cost Avoided via Predictive Planning	Financial value of proactive mitigation

Final Thoughts

In a warming world, climate resilience is no longer a back-office risk management function. It must be embedded into the digital architecture of every organization. Predictive analytics provides the **eyes into the future**, and automation delivers the **hands to act in time**.

By anticipating climate risks before they strike, we do more than survive — we **design for continuity, sustainability, and regeneration**.

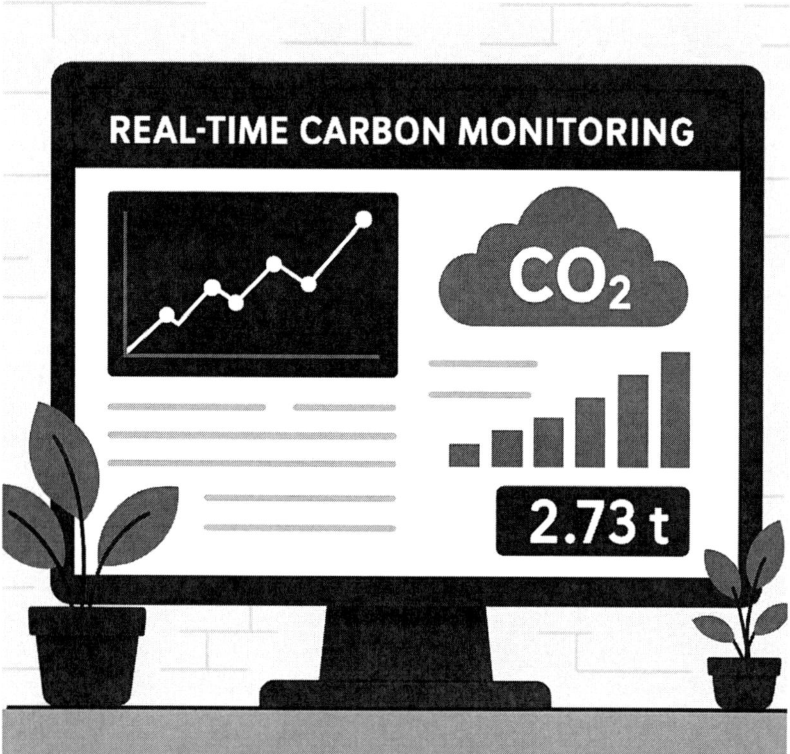
REAL-TIME CARBON MONITORING
CO_2
2.73 t

Chapter 15

Real-Time Carbon Monitoring

"You can't manage what you don't measure — and you can't reduce what you don't track in real time."

Introduction

As organizations commit to Net Zero goals, the ability to **track carbon emissions in real time** has become mission-critical. Annual sustainability reports or spreadsheet-based estimates are no longer sufficient. Real-time carbon monitoring provides the **visibility, accuracy, and responsiveness** required to meet ESG goals, comply with global regulations, and build trust with stakeholders.

This chapter explores how AI, automation, and IoT enable dynamic carbon intelligence across operations, assets, IT infrastructure, and the supply chain.

Why Real-Time Matters

Traditional carbon accounting is:

- Retrospective and slow
- Inaccurate due to manual data inputs
- Disconnected across functions and suppliers

Real-time carbon monitoring shifts the paradigm by:

- Continuously measuring emissions at the source
- Enabling proactive interventions to reduce waste and energy
- Providing transparent dashboards for decision-makers
- Supporting compliance with frameworks like **BRSR, CSRD, SECR, GHG Protocol**

→I→I→I→I→I→I→I

🔍 Real-Life Example: Cloud Operations Emissions

Consider a global financial services company that runs operations on multiple cloud platforms (AWS, Azure, and GCP). Each region's cloud usage contributes significantly to **Scope 2 emissions** — especially during peak compute hours and high cooling loads in data canters.

By deploying **real-time carbon monitoring** using:

- **Microsoft Sustainability Manager** integrated with Azure emissions data
- **Power BI dashboards** for visibility by project, team, and region

- **Automated alerts** to flag carbon-intensive deployments
- **AI-based workload scheduling** that shifts heavy computing to off-peak or greener grid hours

The company **reduced its cloud-related carbon footprint by 23%** in 6 months — without compromising performance.

"By integrating carbon data into **Microsoft Power BI dashboards**, sustainability leaders gain real-time visibility across Scope 1, 2, and 3 metrics."

→I→I→I→I→I→I→I

Enabling Technologies for Carbon Monitoring

Technology	Role in Real-Time Monitoring
IoT Sensors	Capture energy usage, gas emissions, and equipment data
Edge Computing	Analyze data locally for immediate response
Cloud Sustainability Tools	Provide API access to Scope 1, 2, 3 data (Microsoft, SAP)
AI/ML Models	Forecast and optimize emission patterns
Blockchain	Create immutable emission records across the supply chain
Digital Twins	Simulate carbon impact of design or operations

From Data to Decisions – How Automation Helps

Real-time carbon data can trigger automated workflows such as:

- Reducing lighting/HVAC during low occupancy in smart buildings
- Rescheduling manufacturing loads to renewable-heavy grid hours
- Triggering **RPA bots** to alert procurement if a vendor's emission threshold is exceeded
- Auto-generating carbon reports for compliance authorities

→I→I→I→I→I→I→I

KPIs for Real-Time Carbon Monitoring

KPI	Purpose
% Real-Time Visibility Across Scope 1/2/3	Measure how much of emissions are monitored live
Carbon Intensity per Unit Output	Identify hotspots in operations
Automated Alerts per Month	Gauge system responsiveness
GHG Reporting Accuracy (%)	Compare predicted vs actual data
Time to Detect Emissions Spike	Speed of mitigation

→I→I→I→I→I→I→I

Impact on Sustainability Strategy

Real-time carbon monitoring acts as the **nervous system** of a digital sustainability architecture. It ensures:

- **Faster reaction time** to emission anomalies
- **Better decisions** driven by reliable, real-time insights
- **Continuous improvement**, not just year-end corrections
- **Trust and transparency** with stakeholders, regulators, and customers

→|→|→|→|→|→|→|

Final Thoughts

Carbon is no longer an invisible metric hidden in reports. It's a real-time variable that must be embedded into dashboards, decisions, and digital systems. Through real-time carbon monitoring, organizations don't just report on sustainability — they live it every second.

Chapter 16

Governance and Compliance Automation

"Sustainability is not just about goals — it's about governance. Automation ensures it's not optional."

Introduction

Sustainability initiatives often fail not due to lack of intent, but due to a lack of governance. In large organizations, managing ESG compliance, adhering to sustainability frameworks, and tracking progress against targets across departments and geographies can become complex and fragmented.

Governance and compliance automation brings structure, standardization, and accountability into sustainability programs. It ensures that sustainability is not left to interpretation but is embedded into business operations and verified in real time.

→I→I→I→I→I→I→I

The Governance Gap

Organizations face several challenges in governance and sustainability compliance:

- Multiple standards (BRSR, CSRD, GRI, TCFD, etc.)
- Inconsistent data collection across regions and functions
- Manual processes prone to errors and delays
- Lack of ownership and cross-functional alignment

To close this gap, companies are adopting **digital governance frameworks** powered by automation, AI, and integrated ESG platforms.

→I →I →I →I →I →I →I

🔍 Real-Life Example: Automated ESG Reporting in a Multinational

A multinational electronics company with operations in 17 countries struggled to consolidate ESG data for BRSR (India), CSRD (Europe), and internal carbon neutrality goals. Their manual spreadsheets led to late submissions and inaccuracies.

They implemented:

- **Sustainability governance dashboards** using Microsoft Cloud for Sustainability
- **Automated data pipelines** connecting ERP, HRMS, logistics, and utility systems
- **Smart ESG forms** auto-filled by RPA bots
- Real-time **audit trails** for compliance tracking

As a result, the company reduced ESG reporting preparation time by 65% and improved accuracy to over 98%.

→I→I→I→I→I→I→I

Key Components of ESG Governance Automation

Component	Functionality
Policy Engine	Centralizes sustainability standards, rules, and thresholds
Automation Bots	Fill forms, extract data, and submit regulatory reports
AI-Powered Risk Scoring	Identifies compliance gaps and risks proactively
Role-Based Dashboards	Assigns ownership by region, department, or process
Audit Log Generators	Creates immutable trails for regulators and internal reviews
Workflow Engines	Automates approvals, escalations, and documentation routing

Frameworks Supported via Automation

Framework	What Can Be Automated
BRSR (India)	Sustainability indicators, KPIs, and business responsibility
CSRD (EU)	Double materiality, ESG disclosures, taxonomy alignment
GRI/TCFD	Emission, governance, climate risk disclosures
GHG Protocol	Scope 1/2/3 emission calculations

Automation ensures **compliance is embedded**, not reactive.

→|→|→|→|→|→|→|

KPIs for Governance and Compliance Automation

KPI	What It Measures
ESG Data Accuracy (%)	Degree of error-free, validated data
ESG Reporting Cycle Time	Time saved in report generation
% Automated Compliance Workflows	Extent of manual-to-automated transition
Number of Audit Exceptions	Governance effectiveness over time
Regulation Coverage (%)	How many applicable frameworks are integrated

Automation Architecture for ESG Governance

A scalable architecture may include:

- **ERP (SAP/Oracle)** as data source
- **ESG platform (Microsoft, EcoVadis)** as the compliance engine
- **RPA bots** for data extraction, validation, and submission
- **AI models** for identifying gaps and predictive non-compliance
- **Power BI/Tableau** for management dashboards

→|→|→|→|→|→|→|

Final Thoughts

Governance and compliance aren't about red tape — they are about trust, transparency, and transformation. Automation brings the speed, scale, and accuracy needed to govern sustainability in a digital enterprise.

With the right systems in place, organizations can not only meet their ESG obligations but do so efficiently, consistently, and confidently.

Chapter 17

Integrating Renewable Energy Systems

"Digital systems should not just consume clean energy — they should enable it."

Introduction

As the world transitions to net zero, integrating renewable energy sources like **solar, wind, geothermal, and hydro** into business operations has become more than a CSR choice — it's a strategic imperative.

But deploying solar panels or buying renewable energy certificates alone isn't enough. The real value emerges when **digital architecture is used to optimize, automate, and integrate** renewable systems into day-to-day operations, infrastructure, and decision-making.

The Role of Digital in Renewable Energy Integration

Digitally enabled renewable energy integration allows organizations to:

- Monitor and optimize **real-time generation and usage**
- Automate **demand response** and grid interactions
- Simulate energy scenarios using **digital twins**
- Track ROI, emissions offset, and system health
- Enhance visibility across multi-site, multi-source energy flows

→|→|→|→|→|→|→|

🔍 Real-Life Example : Smart Solar Energy Management in Manufacturing

A global manufacturing company installed rooftop solar panels across 12 of its factories. While this reduced emissions, they struggled with:

- Varying generation across geographies
- Grid overload during peak production
- Lack of predictive insight into energy surpluses

They implemented a digital renewable integration strategy:

- Deployed **IoT-based solar inverters** with real-time telemetry
- Used **AI to forecast solar generation** and align with production schedules

- Implemented **battery storage management** and grid sync protocols
- Created dashboards using **Microsoft Sustainability Cloud**

Outcome: They achieved **28% energy cost savings**, reduced CO_2e emissions by 3,200 tons annually, and gained visibility to optimize future renewable investments.

→I→I→I→I→I→I→I

Core Components of a Digital Renewable System

Component	Functionality
Smart Meters + IoT	Measure real-time energy flows, grid sync, surplus discharge
AI/ML Forecasting	Predict renewable availability (solar irradiance, wind speed)
Energy Management System	Balance grid, battery, and demand
Blockchain Contracts	Track and verify green energy trades
Digital Twin Simulations	Model energy performance under future demand scenarios

→I→I→I→I→I→I→I

Renewable Energy Integration in IT and Data Centers

Digital operations (e.g., data centers, edge servers, AI workloads) consume significant energy. Forward-looking organizations now:

- Install **solar microgrids** to power data centers
- Use **software-defined power** to route clean energy dynamically
- Participate in **virtual power purchase agreements (VPPAs)**
- Apply **AI to schedule computing during green energy availability**

This approach ensures that **cloud sustainability** is not just about software — it includes the physical energy behind it.

→I→I→I→I→I→I→I

KPIs for Renewable Energy Integration

KPI	Description
% Energy from Renewable Sources	Renewable penetration into total energy mix
CO_2e Avoided (Tons)	Emission savings through green energy use
Forecast Accuracy of Renewables	Efficiency of AI in managing supply and demand
Battery Storage Utilization (%)	Effectiveness of energy storage systems
Cost per kWh (Blended)	Overall energy cost including renewables and storage

Challenges and How Digital Solves Them

Challenge	Digital Solution
Intermittent generation	AI prediction + smart load balancing
Lack of visibility across sites	Cloud dashboards and IoT integration
Low ROI on solar infrastructure	Simulation with digital twins before investment
Manual reporting and tracking	Automated ledger and blockchain-based certification

→I→I→I→I→I→I→I

Final Thoughts

The integration of renewable energy isn't just about installing clean tech — it's about **orchestrating it intelligently**. Through IoT, AI, automation, and real-time optimization, organizations can move from energy consumers to **active participants in a sustainable grid**.

Digital architecture makes renewable energy **reliable, measurable, and impactful** — all while accelerating the journey to net zero.

Chapter 18

Future Technologies for Decarbonization

"The race to net zero will not be won by doing more of the same — it demands bold, emerging technologies."

Introduction

While current tools like AI, automation, and cloud platforms already deliver significant CO▯ reductions, achieving long-term climate goals requires adopting **next-generation technologies**. These innovations go beyond optimization — they **redefine the foundations** of how we generate energy, manufacture goods, and build digital infrastructure.

This chapter explores the cutting-edge technologies that promise to shape the future of decarbonization across industries.

→I→I→I→I→I→I→I

Why Future Tech Matters in Sustainability

- Today's solutions address **incremental change** — future tech enables **transformational shifts**.
- Hard-to-abate sectors (cement, aviation, steel, cloud compute) require **breakthroughs**, not tweaks.
- Many next-gen technologies are now emerging from R&D into scalable pilots, ready to change how we work.

🔍 Real-Life Example: Direct Air Capture at Data Centers

A cloud service provider partnered with a carbon-tech startup to deploy **Direct Air Capture (DAC)** modules near data centers. These modules:

- Pull ambient air through filters
- Extract CO_2 using electrochemical reactions
- Compress and store captured CO_2 underground or repurpose it

This initiative turned carbon-intensive infrastructure into a **net-positive** system — capturing more CO_2 than it emitted, with all performance insights monitored digitally.

Future Technologies Shaping Decarbonization

Technology	Impact on CO_2 Reduction
Direct Air Capture (DAC)	Removes CO_2 from the atmosphere directly
Green Hydrogen	Powers transport and heavy industry with zero-carbon fuel
Carbon-Aware Computing	Schedules computing when renewable energy is available
AI in Material Innovation	Designs low-carbon materials and processes
Biomanufacturing	Uses microbes to produce chemicals and plastics sustainably
Carbon-Aware Load Shifting	Optimizes energy use based on real-time grid emissions intensity

Role of Digital Architects

As sustainability architects, the role is to:

- Identify **technologies at TRL (Technology Readiness Level) 6–9** for adoption
- Design **hybrid ecosystems** that combine current systems with future tech
- Build **modular, future-ready platforms** to integrate innovation as it matures
- Drive **data transparency** for every carbon-saving claim with auditable records

Enabling the Transition

To accelerate adoption of future decarbonization technologies:

- Leverage **digital twins** to simulate ROI and emission savings before implementation
- Use **blockchain** to certify carbon removal or offsets via DAC and hydrogen projects
- Build open **data exchange standards** to benchmark across vendors and pilots
- Apply **incentive algorithms** (e.g., carbon-aware cloud billing) to change user behavior

KPIs for Future-Tech Integration

KPI	Purpose
CO_2 Captured/Offset via Emerging Tech	Quantifies early-stage impact
Pilot-to-Scale Time	Tracks speed of adoption
Carbon-Aware Compute Utilization (%)	Measures green compute scheduling efficiency
% Energy Supplied by Hydrogen or Biofuel	Transition readiness from fossil-based systems
Innovation ROI per Tonne CO_2	Value gained per unit of CO□ reduced via new technology

Final Thoughts

Decarbonization is not a one-time effort. It's a continuous journey powered by innovation. While today's digital systems provide the backbone for sustainability, it is the **emerging technologies** — carbon-aware computing, DAC, hydrogen, and material innovation — that will define how far and how fast we go.

The responsibility of the modern digital architect is to **design with the future in mind**, building systems that can evolve, scale, and embrace breakthroughs as they arrive.

Chapter 19

Creating a Culture of Sustainability

"Technology can enable change — but culture makes it last."

Introduction

Sustainability is not just a technological transformation; it is a **cultural shift**. The success of green initiatives depends on how deeply sustainability is embedded into the organization's mindset, behaviors, and daily practices.

No amount of automation or AI can replace the power of an engaged workforce, aligned leadership, and a shared purpose. This chapter explores how to **foster a culture of sustainability** — from boardrooms to break rooms — using digital tools, education, and leadership alignment.

Why Culture Matters in Sustainability

Without a strong culture:

- ESG goals remain siloed or performative
- Compliance becomes checkbox-driven, not values-driven
- Innovation slows due to lack of ownership and buy-in
- Greenwashing risks increase

With the right culture:

- Employees become **sustainability ambassadors**
- Every decision reflects environmental and ethical awareness
- Transformation is **self-reinforcing**, not top-down mandated

→|→|→|→|→|→|→|

🔍 Real-Life Example: Gamified Carbon Reduction Program

A European telecom company launched an internal challenge using a mobile app that:

- Tracked employee carbon footprints (commuting, printing, energy use)
- Rewarded low-emission choices with points redeemable for vouchers
- Shared department-wide leaderboards to drive collaboration
- Included digital sustainability training modules

Over 9 months, the initiative saved **over 1,500 tons of CO_2e**, improved employee satisfaction scores, and enhanced ESG transparency in internal reporting.

Pillars of a Sustainability-Driven Culture

Pillar	What It Means in Practice
Leadership Commitment	Executives role-model sustainable decisions
Employee Engagement	Staff involved in idea-generation, reporting, and feedback
Transparency	Dashboards for energy use, emissions, and goals
Digital Nudges	Alerts and rewards to promote eco-friendly behavior
Learning & Development	Regular upskilling on ESG, tools, and regulations

Digital Enablers of Cultural Shift

Tool/Approach	Impact on Culture
Sustainability Portals	Central hub for learning, reporting, and ideas
Gamification Platforms	Make sustainability fun, engaging, and measurable
Digital Recognition	Reward eco-conscious actions visibly (badges, ranks)
ESG Dashboards	Keep everyone informed and aligned
Feedback Loops	Capture ideas, challenges, and innovations from employees

KPIs for Measuring Cultural Impact

KPI	Purpose
% Employee ESG Training Completion	Measures awareness and knowledge penetration
Employee-Generated Sustainability Ideas	Reflects engagement and innovation
Internal Campaign Participation Rate	Tracks voluntary involvement
Culture Index (via surveys)	Gauges alignment with sustainability values
% Sustainable Behaviors Adopted	Changes in energy use, travel, paper, etc.

Embedding Sustainability in Digital Workflows

Culture isn't just slogans — it's visible in daily tools and processes. You can embed sustainability by:

- Adding **CO_2 impact insights** to dashboards and reports
- Making **green alternatives the default** in procurement systems
- Using **digital reminders** to shut down unused equipment
- Creating **cross-functional ESG squads** to champion change

→|→|→|→|→|→|→|

Final Thoughts

A sustainability culture is not built overnight. It grows when organizations align incentives, empower employees, and lead with purpose. Technology can make culture visible — but leaders and teams must bring it to life.

Sustainability becomes real when it's not a project — it's how we work, decide, and live.

Chapter 20

The Road Ahead – A Net Zero Vision

"Sustainability isn't the end of a journey. It's how we design every step forward."

Introduction

As we reach the final chapter of this book, it's important to reflect on one truth: building a sustainable digital future is not a one-time project — it is a **continuous mission**. And the mission is clear — to achieve **net zero emissions**, where the greenhouse gases we produce are equal to or less than those we remove from the atmosphere.

But what does that actually look like in the real world? And how do we, as professionals in digital and technology domains, contribute to this transformation?

The answer lies in **smart architecture**, **bold leadership**, **emerging technology**, and — most importantly — **collective action**.

→|→|→|→|→|→|→|

What is Net Zero?

Net zero means an organization balances the carbon it emits with the carbon it removes or avoids. This includes:

- **Scope 1** emissions – Direct emissions from company-owned sources (like vehicles or factories)
- **Scope 2** – Indirect emissions from purchased electricity
- **Scope 3** – All other indirect emissions (from suppliers, employee travel, product use, etc.)

Achieving net zero requires tackling all three.

→|→|→|→|→|→|→|

🔍 Real-Life Example 1: A Tech Company's Journey

A global software company committed to becoming net zero by 2030. Here's how they made progress:

- **Moved all data centers to renewable energy** sources like wind and solar
- Used **Power BI dashboards** to track real-time energy and carbon data
- Partnered with vendors who reported Scope 3 emissions and had clear reduction goals

- Invested in **carbon removal projects** (like reforestation and direct air capture)

Within 5 years, they reduced over 60% of their carbon footprint — and inspired hundreds of their suppliers to follow suit.

⇥⇥⇥⇥⇥⇥⇥

🔍 Real-Life Example 2: Sustainable E-Commerce Packaging

An e-commerce giant reduced its Scope 3 emissions by **redesigning its packaging system**:

- AI analyzed order sizes and automatically suggested the smallest, most sustainable packaging
- Biodegradable materials replaced plastics
- Delivery routes were optimized using smart logistics tools

This resulted in a **32% reduction in packaging emissions**, while also saving money.

⇥⇥⇥⇥⇥⇥⇥

Four Stages on the Road to Net Zero

Stage	Action Step
1. **Measure Everything**	Use digital tools to track all emissions across Scope 1, 2, and 3
2. **Reduce at the Source**	Replace high-emission systems with clean, efficient alternatives
3. **Automate and Optimize**	Use AI, IoT, and automation to cut waste and improve energy performance
4. **Offset What Remains**	Invest in verified projects that remove or capture CO_2

How Digital Architects Contribute

As a **Sustainability Architect** or **Digital Strategist**, you can drive net zero by:

- Designing **green IT systems** that run on renewable energy
- Creating **vendor selection models** that prioritize ESG criteria
- Embedding **carbon dashboards** into every app, workflow, or report
- Using **digital twins** to model building or product emissions before they are built
- Recommending tools like **Microsoft Sustainability Cloud**, **SAP Green Ledger**, or **IoT-based monitors** to manage energy usage

Your role is not just to make systems work — it is to make systems work sustainably.

⇥⇥⇥⇥⇥⇥⇥

KPIs to Track Net Zero Progress

KPI	What It Tells You
Total CO□e Emissions	Overall carbon footprint from all operations
% Reduction in Scope 3	Success in engaging vendors, partners, and logistics
% Energy from Renewables	Clean energy transition progress
Carbon Intensity per Product	Emissions per unit of service or product delivered
Offset Quality Index	Credibility of carbon offset programs used

Overcoming Common Challenges

Challenge	Solution Using Technology
Hard to track Scope 3 data	Use ESG platforms to gather supplier data digitally
Data scattered across silos	Integrate ESG systems with ERP and reporting tools
Skepticism or lack of engagement	Use gamification, dashboards, and internal campaigns
Cost concerns	Use AI to simulate ROI of energy savings or automation

Final Reflections

We are at a unique point in history.

Climate change is not a distant threat — it's here. But so is our opportunity. Every line of code we write, every system we optimize, and every supplier we choose can help **remove carbon, reduce waste, and regenerate value**.

The **road ahead to net zero** won't be easy. But it's already being built — by professionals like you, in roles like yours.

This book began with systems, but ends with purpose:

You are not just a Digital Architect.

You are a designer of impact.

A builder of trust.

A voice for the future.

Let us all move forward — not just digitally transformed, but **climate-aligned, human-centered, and architected for generations to come**.

Appendix – Author Frameworks

By Satya Prakash, Sustainability Architect

Appendix A: Case Studies in Sustainability Innovation

Case Study 1: Sustainable Agriculture and Water Efficiency

A leading agriculture company in Southeast Asia faced

frequent droughts, leading to water shortages and crop failure. By integrating AI-powered soil moisture sensors and predictive weather analytics, the company optimized irrigation schedules.

- Technology Used: IoT sensors, AI-based climate forecasting
- Result: 35% reduction in water use and a 20% improvement in yield
- Sustainability Impact: Reduced groundwater depletion and carbon emissions from inefficient pumping

→I→I→I→I→I→I→I

Case Study 2 : Cloud Optimization for Digital Sustainability

A global software company adopted a sustainable cloud strategy by migrating to green-certified data centers and shifting workloads to low-carbon intensity regions using AI orchestration.

- Technology Used: Microsoft Cloud for Sustainability, Carbon-aware workload scheduler
- Result: 42% reduction in cloud-related Scope 2 emissions in the first year
- Sustainability Impact: Demonstrated that digital transformation can coexist with emission reduction

→I→I→I→I→I→I→I

Case Study 3 : Sustainable Lighting in Smart Cities

An urban development authority implemented a smart lighting system that used motion detection and daylight sensors across major city zones.

- Technology Used: IoT-enabled LED lighting, RPA for monitoring
- Result: 60% drop in energy consumption from public lighting
- Sustainability Impact: Enhanced urban safety with minimal energy overhead

→|→|→|→|→|→|→|

Case Study 4 : Circular Economy in Consumer Tech

A consumer electronics manufacturer revamped its product lifecycle model. Devices were designed for modular repair, and a reverse logistics system was introduced to collect and recycle end-of-life products.

- Technology Used: Digital twin, blockchain for tracking components
- Result: 70% of returned devices were reused or recycled
- Sustainability Impact: Significant reduction in e-waste and raw material extraction

→|→|→|→|→|→|→|

Case Study 5 : Predictive Carbon Monitoring in Supply Chains

A retail company deployed real-time carbon dashboards to track logistics emissions, using predictive analytics to optimize routing and warehouse energy usage.

- Technology Used: AI route optimization, Power BI carbon dashboard
- Result: 28% reduction in transportation emissions within 12 months

- Sustainability Impact: Empowered procurement and logistics teams to take direct climate action

Case Study 6 : Renewable Energy Integration in Manufacturing

A heavy manufacturing plant shifted from fossil-based energy to solar microgrids combined with battery storage. AI predicted energy loads and balanced grid usage in real time.

- Technology Used: Solar PV, battery storage, AI demand forecasting
- Result: 65% plant power now derived from renewable sources
- Sustainability Impact: Long-term energy cost reduction and GHG savings

Case Study 7 : AI-Driven HVAC Optimization

A large commercial building chain embedded AI-based occupancy sensors and real-time CO_2 monitoring into its HVAC systems.

- Technology Used: Smart HVAC controls, CO_2 sensors, AI energy bots
- Result: 32% energy efficiency improvement in climate control systems
- Sustainability Impact: Lower indoor pollution and energy intensity per square foot

The following frameworks were designed to guide enterprises, architects, and technologists toward practical, measurable, and strategic sustainability in digital ecosystems. Each model is original and created by the author for this book.

→|→|→|→|→|→|→|

◈ 1. The 5P Framework for Cloud Sustainability

A strategic model for evaluating and optimizing cloud workloads for environmental impact.

Pillar	Focus Area
Provider	Select cloud vendors committed to renewable energy and carbon transparency
Platform	Choose cloud-native or serverless services for better efficiency
Placement	Deploy workloads in low-carbon, water-efficient regions
Performance	Right-size and optimize workloads to minimize resource consumption
Policy	Establish governance to monitor emissions, automate sustainability, and enforce green usage patterns

"You may not own the cloud's hardware, but you own the impact of your architecture."

— Satya Prakash (© 2025)

→|→|→|→|→|→|→|

◈ 2. The S.A.A.S. Vendor Checklist

A decision-making tool for selecting environmentally responsible SaaS partners.

S – Source	**Where is the SaaS hosted, and how green is its infrastructure?**
A – Architecture	Is the solution designed for efficient compute, storage, and bandwidth?
A – Accountability	Does the vendor disclose emissions, follow ESG standards, and track CO_2?
S – Sustainability	Is the vendor actively pursuing a decarbonization or net-zero agenda?

"When you onboard a SaaS vendor, you're also onboarding their carbon decisions."

— Satya Prakash (© 2025)

◈ 3. The R.O.A.D. Framework for Automation Sustainability

A four-step approach to building automation systems that reduce waste and optimize resource use.

Step	Action
R – Recognize	Identify high-consumption, low-efficiency processes
O – Optimize	Improve design, timing, or flow to reduce waste
A – Automate	Use intelligent automation to sustain optimizations reliably
D – Decarbonize	Measure impact, offset emissions, and align with sustainability targets